THE USER GENERATED CONTENT CREATOR'S HANDBOOK

How to Turn Your Passion for UGC content into a Successful Career

INTRODUCTION

UGC stands for "user-generated content." It refers to any type of content that is created and shared by users of a website, social media platform, or other online community. This can include text, photos, videos, and other types of media. User-generated content can be created for a variety of reasons, including sharing personal experiences, opinions, or ideas with others, to engage with a community, or to contribute to a conversation or debate. It can also be created for entertainment or creative expression. User-generated content (also known as UGC or consumer-generated content) is original, brand-specific content created by customers and published on social media or other channels. It is an important aspect of many online communities and can contribute to the vibrancy and diversity of the content available. It is often seen as more authentic and relatable than content created by brands or organizations, and can be a useful source of ideas and feedback for companies and organizations. User-generated content (UGC) is created by users of a website, social media platform, or other online community. It can take many forms, including text, photos, videos, and other types of media.

There are a variety of ways that people create user-generated content. Some common methods include:

Sharing personal experiences, opinions, or ideas:

This can include writing blog posts, posting on social media, or sharing photos or videos of personal experiences or events.

Engaging with a community:

This can include participating in discussions, leaving comments on other people's posts, or contributing to online forums or groups.

Creating content for entertainment or creative expression:

This can include creating memes, drawing or painting, or making videos or music.

Contributing to a conversation or debate:

This can include sharing information or research, or expressing an opinion on a particular topic.

Overall, user-generated content is a way for people to share their thoughts, experiences, and creativity with others online.

User-generated content can be a powerful marketing tool for businesses and organizations. By encouraging customers or fans to create and share content related to their products or services, companies can tap into the authenticity and influence of their user base. User-generated content can also be a valuable source of information and ideas for businesses. By listening to and engaging with their customers and fans, companies can get valuable feedback and insights that can help them improve their products or services. It's important for businesses and organizations to have clear guidelines and policies in place for user-generated content. This can help to ensure that the content aligns with the values and goals of the company, and that it doesn't violate any laws or regulations. It can be a powerful way for individuals to share their experiences and ideas with others. It can also be a way for people to connect with like-minded individuals and build online communities. User-generated content can be created using a wide range of tools and technologies, including smartphones, cameras, video editing software, and audio recording equipment which can be created for a variety of purposes, including personal expression, entertainment, education, and activism. . By encouraging users to create and share content, companies can tap into the influence and authenticity of their user base as well as it being a valuable source of information and ideas for businesses and organizations. By listening to and engaging with their customers and fans, companies can get valuable feedback and insights that can help them improve their products or services.

It's important for businesses and organizations to have clear guidelines and policies in place for user-generated content. This can help to ensure that the content aligns with the values and goals of the company, and that it doesn't violate any laws or regulations. User-generated content can be shared on a variety of platforms, including social media, blogs, forums, and online marketplaces.

User-generated content can be a great way for people to express themselves creatively and share their talents with the world. There is no one-size-fits-all format for user-generated content (UGC) creation, as UGC can

Social media posts: Users can create and share content on social media platforms such as Facebook, Twitter, and Instagram. This can include everything from personal updates and photos to memes and news articles.

Online forum posts: Users can contribute to online discussions and debates by posting in forums or discussion groups.

Creative projects: Users can share creative projects such as artwork, music, or writing on platforms like DeviantArt or Etsy.

The best type of content will depend on the goals and audience of the UGC creator. That being said, some types of UGC tend to be more popular and effective than others. Here are a few examples of types of UGC that are often well-received by audiences:

Authentic and personal content: UGC that is authentic, genuine, and personal tends to be well-received by audiences. This can include personal stories, experiences, or opinions, as well as candid photos or videos.

Engaging and interactive content: UGC that is interactive and engaging can be a great way to build a sense of community around a brand or topic. This can include social media posts that encourage users to like, comment, or share, or content that asks for user input or feedback.

Educational or informative content: UGC that provides valuable information or insights can be a great way to build trust and credibility with an audience. This can include tutorial videos, how-to guides, or expert insights.

Humorous or entertaining content: UGC that is funny or entertaining can be a great way to engage and delight an audience. This can include memes, jokes, or humorous video content.

Overall, the best type of UGC is often content that is authentic, engaging, and valuable to the audience. By creating content that resonates with your audience and meets their needs, you can build a strong and engaged community around your content.

HOW TO CREATE A NICHE FOR YOURSELF AS A UGC CREATOR

Deciding on a niche for yourself as a user-generated content (UGC) creator can be a challenging but important task. Here are a few steps you can take to help you determine your niche:

Identify your interests and passions:

What are you most interested in or passionate about? Consider what topics or subjects you enjoy learning about or spending time on.

Consider your skills and expertise:

What skills or knowledge do you have that you can share with others? Think about the things you are good at or have experience in.

Research your audience demographics:

Who are you creating content for? Consider the demographics and interests of your potential audience, as well as what types of content they are likely to be interested in.

Evaluate your competition:

Look at the other UGC creators in your chosen niche and see what they are doing. Consider how you can differentiate yourself and offer something unique or valuable to your audience.

Test your ideas:

Once you have identified a few potential niches, try creating some content in those areas and see how it is received. You can use social media or other online platforms to get feedback and see what resonates with your audience.

Look for areas where there is a demand for content:

Consider whether there is a demand for content in your chosen niche. This can help to ensure that your content will be seen and appreciated by your audience.

Find a niche that allows you to be creative:

Choose a niche that allows you to express your creativity and share your unique perspective. This can help to make the process of creating content more enjoyable and fulfilling.

Be willing to adapt and evolve:

Your niche may change over time as your interests and skills evolve. Be open to exploring new areas and adapting your content to meet the needs and interests of your audience.

Consider your long-term goals:

Think about where you want to go with your content and how your chosen niche fits into those plans. This can help you to focus your efforts and stay motivated as you work towards your goals.

By taking the time to carefully consider your niche, you can identify a niche that aligns with your interests, skills, and audience that you are excited to create content for and you can set yourself up for success as a UGC creator and build a strong and engaged audience.

BUILDING YOUR ONLINE PRESENCE
TIPS AND STRATEGIES FOR SOCIAL MEDIA SUCCESS

In today's digital world, having a strong online presence is essential for success as a user-generated content creator. Social media platforms such as Instagram, TikTok, and YouTube offer a wide range of tools and features that can help you connect with your audience and promote your content. Here are a few key strategies for building your online presence on social media:

Choose the right platforms: Not all social media platforms are created equal, and it's important to choose the ones that are most relevant to your niche and target audience. For example, if you're focused on visual content, platforms like Instagram and TikTok might be a good fit, while YouTube is a great option for video content.

Create a consistent brand identity: Your social media profiles and content should reflect your personal brand and aesthetic. This includes using consistent colors, fonts, and imagery across all of your profiles, as well as crafting a clear and consistent messaging.

Engage with your audience: Social media is all about building connections and relationships, so it's important to regularly engage with your followers. This could include responding to comments and messages, sharing user-generated content, and running polls or quizzes to encourage participation.

Utilize hashtags: Hashtags can help you reach a wider audience and connect with others in your niche. Use relevant hashtags in your posts and stories, and consider creating your own branded hashtag to encourage your audience to share their own content.

Use social media analytics: Most social media platforms offer built-in analytics tools that can help you understand your audience and track the performance of your content. Use these tools to identify what's working and what's not, and adjust your strategy accordingly.

Collaborate with other creators: Partnering with other creators can help you reach a new audience and bring fresh perspectives to your content. Look for opportunities to collaborate with other creators in your niche, and consider reaching out to influencers or brands that align with your values and aesthetic.

HOW TO UTILIZE VARIOUS SOCIAL MEDIA PLATFORMS FOR USER-GENERATED CONTENTS

Instagram

This visual-based platform is ideal for showcasing User - generated photos and videos, particularly those that are visually appealing or showcase products or services in a creative way. If you're a creator looking to share user-generated content (UGC) on Instagram, here are some tips to help you get started, by following these tips, you can effectively share user-generated content on Instagram and grow your following and engagement.

1. Research and identify popular hashtags related to your niche. This will help you reach a larger audience and make it easier for people to discover your content.

2. Use relevant hashtags in your posts and captions. This will help your content show up in relevant searches and make it more visible to your target audience.

3. Engage with other users and communities. This can help you build relationships, gain exposure, and get more user-generated content for your own feed.

4. Collaborate with other creators or brands. This can help you reach a wider audience and get more user-generated content for your feed.

5. Encourage your followers to share their own content with you. This can help you get more user-generated content and give your followers a sense of ownership and engagement with your content.

6. Keep an eye on Instagram's terms of service. Make sure you're following all of the rules and guidelines when it comes to using user-generated content on the platform.

TikTok

This short-form video platform is great for showcasing user-generated content that is fun, entertaining, or informative. Make sure you're following all of the rules and guidelines when it comes to using user-generated content on the platform. Use creative and engaging video editing techniques. TikTok is known for its creative and entertaining videos, so make sure your content stands out by using interesting transitions, music, and effects. Make use of TikTok's features, such as stickers, filters, and effects. These features can help your content stand out and make it more visually appealing. Use the "For You" page to your advantage. This page is where many users discover new content, so make sure your videos are optimized to show up there by using relevant hashtags and engaging with other users. It's also important to keep in mind that TikTok has a younger audience, so your content should be age-appropriate and aligned with the platform's community guidelines.

Here are a few additional tips to help you succeed on TikTok as a UGC creator:

1. Be consistent with your posting schedule. This will help you build an audience and keep them engaged with your content.

2. Engage with your followers and other users. This can help you build relationships and create a sense of community around your content.

3. Share behind-the-scenes content and personal stories. TikTok users tend to enjoy seeing the "real" side of creators, so sharing personal stories or glimpses into your life can help you connect with your audience.

4. Experiment with different formats and types of content. TikTok is known for its creative and varied content, so try out different formats and styles to see what works best for you.

Twitter

This platform is known for its fast-paced, conversational nature, making it a good choice for sharing user-generated content that is timely or relevant to current events. If you're a creator looking to share user-generated content (UGC) on Twitter, here are some tips to help you get started, by following these tips, you can effectively share user-generated content on Twitter and grow your following and engagement.

1. Research and identify popular hashtags related to your niche. This will help you reach a larger audience and make it easier for people to discover your content.

2. Use relevant hashtags in your tweets and captions. This will help your content show up in relevant searches and make it more visible to your target audience.

3. Engage with other users and communities. This can help you build relationships, gain exposure.

4. Collaborate with other creators or brands. This can help you get your work in front of the right brands.

5. Keep an eye on Twitter's terms of service. Make sure you're following all of the rules and guidelines when it comes to using user-generated content on the platform.

YouTube

This video platform is perfect for sharing user-generated content that is more in-depth or educational, as it allows creators to post longer videos and provide more information. If you're a creator looking to share user-generated content (UGC) on YouTube, here are some tips to help you get started. Research and identify popular keywords and topics related to your niche. This will help you optimize your titles and descriptions and make it easier for brands to discover your content. Use relevant keywords and tags in your videos and descriptions. This will help your content show up in relevant searches and make it more visible to your target audience.

Facebook

This platform is great for sharing user-generated content that is more personal or emotional, as it allows users to create and join groups centered around specific interests or causes. If you're a creator looking to share user-generated content (UGC) on Facebook, here are some tips to help you get started. Research and identify popular hashtags and groups related to your niche. This will help you reach a larger audience and make it easier for brands to discover your content.

Pinterest

This visual-based platform is ideal for sharing user-generated content that is creative, informative, or inspiring, as it allows users to create and share collections of images and ideas. Research and identify popular keywords and topics related to your niche. This will help you optimize your titles and descriptions and make it easier for people to discover your content. Use relevant keywords and tags in your pins and descriptions. This will help your content show up in relevant searches and make it more visible to your target audience. Engage with other users and communities. This can help you build relationships, gain exposure, and get more user-generated content for your own profile. Keep posting original and creative content, the more people engage with your content, the more pinterest will push it out to those kinds of people making you easy to find by brands. Keep an eye on Pinterest's terms of service. Make sure you're following all of the rules and guidelines when it comes to using user-generated content on the platform.

LinkedIn

This professional networking platform is a good choice for sharing user-generated content that is business-related or industry-specific, as it allows users to connect with other professionals in their field. LinkedIn is a professional networking platform that can be a useful tool for finding user-generated content (UGC) jobs. Here are some tips to help you get started:

1. Create a strong LinkedIn profile. Your profile should showcase your skills, experience, and accomplishments, as well as any relevant education or certifications.

2. Join relevant LinkedIn groups. There are many groups on LinkedIn focused on specific industries or topics, and joining these groups can help you connect with other professionals and potentially find UGC jobs.

3. Connect with other professionals in your field. Building a strong network on LinkedIn can help you learn about new opportunities and get recommendations for UGC jobs.

4. Use LinkedIn's job search feature. This feature allows you to search for jobs by location, industry, and other criteria. You can also set up job alerts to receive notifications when new UGC jobs are posted that match your interests.

5. Use LinkedIn's publishing platform to share your own UGC content. This can help you showcase your skills and abilities and potentially attract the attention of potential clients or employers.

It's important to remember that different platforms will work better for different types of user-generated content, and that it's important to consider the specific goals and audience of your content when choosing which platform to use.

HOW TO CREATE UGC

User-generated content (UGC) is any type of content that is created and shared by users, rather than by a professional organization or brand. This can include photos, videos, text, audio, or other types of media that are created and shared by individuals on social media, blogs, forums, or other online platforms.

To create UGC content, you will need to follow these steps:

1. Choose a topic or theme. Consider what you want to create content about and how it will be relevant and engaging to your audience.

2. Use a content creation tool. Depending on the type of UGC you want to create, you may need to use a specific tool such as a camera for photography, a video editing software for videography, or a design software for design work.

3. Create the content. Use your chosen content creation tool to create the UGC content, following any guidelines or requirements you have set for yourself or been given by a client.

4. Edit and refine the content. Review the content you have created and make any necessary edits or refinements to ensure that it is of high quality and meets your standards.

5. Share the content. Once you are satisfied with your UGC content, share it on social media, your blog, or other online platforms to get it seen by your audience.

CREATING A VIDEO AD

Creating video ads for brands can be a rewarding and challenging task. As a UGC creator, creating video ads for brands involves creating video content that promotes a brand's products or services to a target audience. This typically involves working with the brand to understand their target audience and the message they want to convey, and using your creative skills to produce a video ad that resonates with the audience and effectively communicates the brand's message. As a UGC creator, you may be responsible for writing the script, shooting and editing the video, and ensuring that the final product meets the brand's standards and objectives. Creating video ads for brands can be a challenging task, but it can also be a rewarding way to use your skills and creativity to help businesses promote their products and services to a wider audience. Understand the brand's target audience and message. Before you start creating the video ad, make sure you understand the brand's target audience and the message they want to convey. This will help you create a video ad that resonates with the audience and effectively communicates the brand's message.

Keep the video ad short and to the point. Video ads should be short and to the point, as people are generally not willing to watch long ads. Aim for a video ad that is 30 seconds to one minute long.

Use a clear and compelling call to action. Your video ad should include a clear and compelling call to action that tells the viewer what they should do next. This could be visiting the brand's website, signing up for a newsletter, or purchasing a product.

Use high-quality visuals and sound. The visuals and sound in your video ad should be of high quality to keep the viewer engaged and interested.

Test and optimize the video ad. After you create the video ad, test it with a small group to see how it performs. Based on the feedback, make any necessary changes to optimize the ad's performance.

UGC SCRIPTWRITING

UGC scriptwriting is the process of writing scripts for user-generated content (UGC) such as videos, podcasts, or live streams. As a UGC scriptwriter, you may be responsible for creating the script for a video or audio production, outlining the key points, dialog, and action that will be featured in the final product.

To write a UGC script, you will need to follow these steps:

1. Understand the purpose and goals of the UGC. Before you start writing the script, make sure you understand the purpose and goals of the UGC and how it will be used. This will help you create a script that effectively communicates the desired message to the audience.

2. Research the topic. Gather information and research the topic you will be covering in the UGC to ensure that the script is accurate and informative.

3. Outline the key points and structure of the script. Organize the information you have gathered into a clear and logical structure, and outline the key points that you want to cover in the UGC.

4. Write the script. Use your outline to write the script, focusing on creating a clear and engaging narrative that will keep the audience interested and engaged.

5. Edit and revise the script. Review the script and make any necessary edits or revisions to ensure that it is clear, concise, and free of errors.

HOW TO GET UGC JOBS

Here are some tips to help you find user-generated content (UGC) jobs:

Create a strong online presence.

Having a professional website or online portfolio can help you showcase your work and make it easier for potential clients to find you.

Build a strong personal brand.

Your personal brand is the reputation you build for yourself based on your skills, abilities, and values. By establishing a strong personal brand, you can differentiate yourself from other UGC creators and make yourself more attractive to potential clients.

Stay up-to-date with industry trends and techniques.

UGC is a constantly evolving field, so it's important to stay informed about new trends and techniques in order to stay competitive and offer valuable services to clients.

Build a strong portfolio.

Having a portfolio of your work will help potential clients or employers see your skills and abilities and understand what you can offer.

Network with other professionals.

Building relationships with other professionals in your field can help you learn about new opportunities and potentially get recommendations for UGC jobs.

Use online job boards and websites.

There are many websites and job boards that specialize in UGC jobs, such as Upwork, Fiverr, and PeoplePerHour. These platforms allow you to find and apply for UGC jobs from clients all over the world.

Use social media to your advantage.

LinkedIn, Twitter, and other social media platforms can be useful tools for finding UGC jobs. Use them to showcase your work, engage with other professionals, and learn about new opportunities.

Reach out to potential clients directly.

If you have a specific company or client in mind that you'd like to work with, don't be afraid to reach out and pitch your services directly.

Be open to working with clients of all sizes.

UGC jobs can come in all shapes and sizes, from small one-off projects to long-term contracts with major brands. By being open to working with a wide range of clients, you can build a diverse portfolio and gain valuable experience.

MONETIZING YOUR USER-GENERATED CONTENT: OPTIONS AND STRATEGIES

As a user-generated content creator, you may be interested in monetizing your content and turning your passion into a source of income. There are a number of options available for monetizing your content, and it's important to find the strategies that work best for you and your audience. Here are a few key options to consider:

Sponsorships and partnerships: One of the most common ways to monetize your content is through sponsorships and partnerships with brands and companies. This could include sponsored content, sponsored social media posts, or sponsored events or experiences.

Advertising: If you have a large and engaged audience, you may be able to monetize your content through advertising. This could include running ads on your social media profiles or blog, or partnering with ad networks to place ads on your content.

Affiliate marketing: Affiliate marketing involves promoting products or services on behalf of a company and earning a commission for any resulting sales. This can be a great way to monetize your content if you have a loyal and engaged audience that trusts your recommendations.

Patreon: Patreon is a platform that allows creators to receive ongoing support from their audience through monthly donations. This can be a great way to monetize your content if you have a dedicated and loyal following.

Selling products or services: If you have a unique skill or expertise, you may be able to monetize your content by selling products or services related to your niche. This could include e-books, courses, consulting services, or physical products.

Subscription models: Some creators monetize their content through subscription models, where users pay a fee to access exclusive content or perks. This can be a good option if you have a large and engaged audience and are able to consistently produce high-quality content.

By exploring these options and finding the strategies that work best for you and your audience, you'll be well on your way to monetizing your user-generated content and turning your passion into a sustainable source of income. Remember to stay true to your values and be transparent with your audience about your monetization strategies, and you'll be able to build a successful and fulfilling career as a user-generated content creator.

BUILDING A UGC PORTFOLIO

Choose a focus for your portfolio. Your portfolio should showcase your skills and abilities in a specific area of UGC, such as photography, videography, design, or writing. Include a variety of your best work. Your portfolio should include a range of different types of UGC that you have created, such as photos, videos, designs, or articles. Organize your portfolio in a clear and concise manner. Your portfolio should be easy to navigate and should highlight your best work in a way that is easy for potential clients or employers to understand. Include detailed descriptions of your projects. Each piece of UGC in your portfolio should include a detailed description of what it is and what you did to create it. This will help potential clients or employers understand your process and the value you bring to the table. Use a professional design. Your portfolio should look professional and polished, so make sure to use high-quality images and a clean, modern design. Regularly update your portfolio. As you create new UGC, be sure to add it to your portfolio so that it stays up-to-date and reflects your current skills and abilities. Use a consistent style.

Choose a consistent style for your portfolio, whether it's a cohesive color scheme, a consistent font, or a similar layout for each piece of UGC. This will help your portfolio look cohesive and professional.

Customize your portfolio for different audiences. Depending on the type of UGC jobs you're seeking, you may want to tailor your portfolio to appeal to different types of clients or employers. For example, if you're looking for corporate clients, you may want to include more professional-looking content, whereas if you're targeting a younger audience, you may want to showcase more creative or edgy work.

Get feedback from others. Ask for feedback from other UGC professionals, clients, or friends and family to get a fresh perspective on your portfolio and see if there are any areas you can improve.

TOOLS YOU WILL NEED TO GET STARTED WITH UGC

A content creation tool. Depending on the type of UGC you create, you may need a specific tool such as a camera for photography, video editing software for videography, or a design software for design work. A computer or device with a internet connection. You will need a device that you can use to create and edit your UGC and upload it to your portfolio.

A portfolio platform. There are many platforms you can use to create and host your UGC portfolio, such as Behance, Carbonmade, or WordPress. Choose a platform that is easy to use and allows you to showcase your work in a professional and visually appealing way. You may also need to get a domain name and hosting plan (optional). If you want to create a custom website for your portfolio, you will need to purchase a domain name and hosting plan from a provider such as GoDaddy or HostGator.

Canva is a design tool that can be useful for building a user-generated content (UGC) portfolio. Use Canva's templates to create visually appealing layouts for your

UGC. Canva offers a wide range of templates that you can use to create professional-looking designs for your portfolio, such as blog post templates, social media graphics, and presentation slides. Use Canva's design elements to add style and polish to your UGC. Canva offers a wide range of design elements, such as shapes, lines, icons, and images, that you can use to add visual interest to your portfolio. Use Canva's export and sharing options to publish your portfolio. Once you've created your UGC portfolio using Canva, you can easily export and share it with others. By using Canva to create and publish your UGC portfolio, you can create a professional-looking portfolio that showcases your skills and abilities and helps you stand out in the field,

HOW TO FIND CLIENTS

Social media can be a powerful tool for finding user-generated content (UGC) jobs. Here are some tips to help you use social media to get UGC jobs:

Use LinkedIn to connect with other professionals in your field.
LinkedIn is a professional networking platform that can be a useful tool for finding UGC jobs. Use it to build relationships with other professionals, showcase your work, and learn about new opportunities.

Use Twitter to find job openings and engage with other professionals.

Twitter is a great platform for finding job openings and connecting with other professionals in your field. Use hashtags related to your industry and UGC to find job openings and engage with other professionals.

Use Instagram to showcase your work and connect with potential clients.

Instagram is a visual platform that can be a useful tool for showcasing your UGC and connecting with potential clients. Use hashtags and engage with other users to get your work seen and build relationships.

Use Facebook to connect with other professionals and join relevant groups.

Facebook has many groups focused on specific industries or topics, and joining these groups can help you connect with other professionals and potentially find UGC jobs.

Use Upwork and Fiverr

Upwork and fiverr are platforms that allows freelancers to find and apply for a wide range of jobs, including user-generated content (UGC) gigs. Upwork for example: your Upwork profile is essentially your resume, so make sure it showcases your skills and experience in a clear and concise manner. Include a portfolio of your work and any relevant education or certifications. It allows you to select categories and subcategories that reflect your skills and expertise, so make sure you choose the ones that best fit your UGC skills. You can use keywords to help clients find freelancers who fit their needs, so make sure you include relevant keywords in your profile and proposals to increase your chances of being found.

Tailor your proposals to each client. Each client's needs and preferences are different, so make sure to tailor your proposals to each client and highlight the specific skills and experience that make you a good fit for their project. Your gig descriptions should also clearly describe the UGC services you offer and the value you bring to the table. Make sure to include details about your process, turnaround time, and any additional services you offer.

Engage with clients and respond promptly. Upwork allows you to communicate with clients directly, so make sure to engage with them and respond promptly to their messages. This will help you build relationships and increase your chances of getting hired.

COLLABORATING WITH BRANDS AND COMPANIES

Collaborating with brands and companies can be a great way to grow your audience, monetize your content, and expand your reach as a user-generated content creator. However, it's important to approach these collaborations carefully and ensure that they align with your values and goals. Here are a few key strategies for collaborating with brands and companies:

Research potential partners: Before reaching out to brands and companies, it's important to do your research and identify potential partners that align with your values and audience. Look for companies that have a track record of working with creators, and consider their reputation and values to ensure that the partnership is a good fit.

Negotiate terms and conditions: When working with brands and companies, it's important to clearly define the terms and conditions of the collaboration. This should include the scope of the partnership, the compensation or benefits you will receive, and any other relevant details. Make sure to put these terms in writing to avoid misunderstandings or disputes down the road.

Be transparent: It's important to be transparent with your audience about your collaborations and disclose any sponsored or sponsored content. This will help you maintain trust and credibility with your audience.

UGC EMAIL PROPOSAL

An UGC email proposal is an email that is sent to a potential client or brand to pitch a user-generated content (UGC) project or collaboration. UGC email proposals are typically used by freelancers or creative agencies to propose UGC services to potential clients and outline the scope, timeline, and budget for the project. To create effective user-generated content (UGC) proposals, you will need to follow these steps:

1. Understand the client's needs and goals: Before you start creating the proposal, make sure you understand the client's needs and goals for the UGC project. This will help you create a proposal that addresses their specific needs and aligns with their objectives.

2. Research the client and their industry: Gather information about the client and their industry to ensure that you are creating a proposal that is relevant and tailored to their needs.

3. Write the proposal: Use the information you have gathered to create a clear and concise proposal that outlines the scope, timeline, and budget for the project,

and explains the value that you will bring to the collaboration.

4. An introduction: This should include your name and company (if applicable), and a brief overview of your UGC services.

5. A description of the UGC project: This should include details about the scope of the project, the goals and objectives of the UGC, and any specific requirements or constraints. Clearly outline the scope of the UGC project, including the type of content that will be created.

6. A timeline: This should outline the timeline for the project, including when the UGC will be created and delivered to the client.

7. A budget: Determine the budget for the project, including any fees or expenses that the client will need to cover. This should outline the budget for the project, including any fees or expenses that the client will need to cover.

8. A call to action: This should include a clear and compelling call to action that tells the client what they

should do next, such as schedule a call or request a proposal.

9. Review and revise the proposal: Review the proposal and make any necessary edits or revisions to ensure that it is clear, concise, and free of errors.

By including these elements in your UGC email proposal, you can effectively pitch your UGC services to potential clients and set the stage for a successful collaboration.

UGC INTERVIEWS

After sending an email, you might get a reply from brands wanting to either have a chat, jump on a phone call or a zoom call, this is what you'll call a UGC interview. This helps them to decide whether you are a best fit for their marketing goals

As a UGC creator, you may be invited to participate in UGC interviews with brands as a way to gather insights and perspectives from real people about the brand's products or services. During these interviews, the brand may ask you questions about your experiences with their products or services, your opinions on the brand, and any suggestions or feedback you have. It's important to be honest and authentic in your responses and to provide valuable insights and perspectives that can help the brand improve their products or services. It's also important to be respectful and professional, and to follow any guidelines or rules that the brand has set for the interview. You can help the brand gather valuable insights and feedback from real customers, and use your creativity and skills to contribute to the development of the brand's products or services.

Here are some tips to help you ace the interview and provide valuable insights and perspectives:

Prepare for the interview:

Review the list of questions or topics that the brand will be asking about, and spend some time thinking about your experiences and opinions on these topics.

Be honest and authentic:

During the interview, be honest and authentic in your responses, and don't be afraid to share your thoughts and opinions even if they are critical of the brand.

Provide valuable insights and perspectives:

Offer valuable insights and perspectives on the brand's products or services, and share any suggestions or feedback that you think could help the brand improve.

Be respectful and professional:

Be respectful and professional in your interactions with the brand, and follow any guidelines or rules that they have set for the interview.

HOW TO NEGOTIATE PROFITABLE PRICES FOR YOUR SERVICES

As a UGC creator, you may be approached by brands to create user-generated content (UGC) for their products or services. When negotiating UGC prices for your services with brands, it's important to consider your skills, experience and the value you are bringing to the project, and to communicate this value clearly and effectively to the brand. As a user-generated content (UGC) creator, it's important to establish clear pricing for your services to ensure that you are fairly compensated for your work. Here are some tips to help you negotiate UGC prices with brands:

Research the market: Research the going rates for UGC services in your industry to get a sense of what you can expect to charge for your work.

Determine your value: Consider the value that you bring to the table as a UGC creator, including your skills, experience, and unique perspective.

Establish a base rate: Establish a base rate for your UGC services that reflects the value you bring to the table and is in line with market rates.

Consider the scope of the project: Take into account the scope of the project, including the amount of time and effort that will be required to complete the UGC, when determining your prices.

Set clear terms: Make sure to set clear terms and conditions for the project, including any payment schedules or deadlines, to avoid misunderstandings or disputes.

Negotiate with the brand: When negotiating with a brand, be prepared to discuss your base rate and any additional fees or expenses that may be associated with the project. Be open to negotiating and be willing to compromise, but also be firm about what you are worth and what you are willing to accept. During the negotiation process, be open to discussing the brand's budget and your pricing, and try to come to an agreement that is fair and reasonable for both parties.

THE UGC CONTRACT

A UGC contract is a legal document that outlines the terms and conditions of a user-generated content (UGC) project between a creator and a brand. UGC contracts can be used for a variety of purposes, including protecting the rights and interests of both parties, setting clear expectations and boundaries for the project, and avoiding misunderstandings or disputes. A UGC contract can help protect both parties by setting clear expectations and boundaries for the project, and can help avoid misunderstandings or disputes.

To draft a UGC contract for a brand you work with, you will need to include the following elements:

Parties: Identify the brand and the UGC creator as the parties to the contract.

Scope of work: Clearly outline the scope of the UGC project, including the type of content that will be created, the goals and objectives of the UGC, and any specific requirements or constraints.

Timeline: Include a timeline for the project, including when the UGC will be created and delivered to the brand.

Budget: Outline the budget for the project, including any fees or expenses that the brand will need to cover.

Intellectual property: Specify who will own the intellectual property rights for the UGC, and whether the brand will have the right to use the UGC in any way.

Termination: Include provisions for terminating the contract in the event that either party fails to fulfill their obligations under the contract.

These simple but important things to look out for will help you create a clear, concise and profitable ugc contract for both parties. Brands will sometimes give you their own ugc contract, be sure to go through it with a legal professional to understand the nitty gritty involed especially if the contract will be for a long time, you do not want to be tied to a bad contract. If you do not get a contract from them and they are retained customers, try to draft up your own contract and pitch it to them.

COMMON MISTAKES THAT UGC CREATORS MAKE

Here are some common mistakes that UGC creators may make:

Not Understanding the Brand's Goals and Objectives

It's important for UGC creators to understand the brand's goals and objectives for the UGC project in order to create content that aligns with these objectives.

Not Following the Brand's Guidelines

Many brands have specific guidelines for UGC, such as tone, style, or content requirements. It's important for UGC creators to follow these guidelines to ensure that the content they create is in line with the brand's expectations.

Not Getting Permission to Use Third-Party Content

If you are using third-party content in your UGC, it's important to get permission from the copyright holder before using it. Failure to do so can result in legal issues.

Not Being Transparent About Sponsored Content

If you are creating sponsored content for a brand, it's important to be transparent about the fact that the content is sponsored. Failure to disclose this information can result in legal issues and damage your credibility as a creator.

Not Owning the Rights to the Content

As a UGC creator, it's important to own the rights to the content you create, or to have permission from the copyright holder to use it. Otherwise, you may be infringing on someone else's intellectual property rights.

Not Having a Clear Call to Action

A call to action is an instruction that tells the viewer what to do next, such as visiting a website or purchasing a product. It's important for UGC creators to include a clear call to action in their content to encourage the viewer to take the desired action.

Not Optimizing For Social Media Platforms

Different social media platforms have different guidelines and best practices for content creation. It's important for UGC creators to optimize their content for the specific platform they are using in order to maximize its reach and impact.

Not Engaging With the Audience

Engaging with the audience is an important part of building a following and maintaining a strong presence on social media. UGC creators should make an effort to respond to comments, questions, and feedback from their audience to foster a sense of community and build relationships with their followers.

Not Leveraging Hashtags

Hashtags are a powerful tool for increasing the reach and visibility of your content on social media. UGC creators should include relevant hashtags in their content to help their content reach a wider audience.

Not Keeping Up With the Latest Trends

The world of social media is constantly evolving, and it's important for UGC creators to stay up to date with the latest trends and best practices in order to create effective and engaging content.

BUILDING A SUSTAINABLE CAREER AS A USER-GENERATED CONTENT CREATOR

Building a successful and sustainable career as a user-generated content creator requires a combination of hard work, creativity, and business savvy. Here are a few key strategies for building a long-term career in this field, by following these strategies and tips, you'll be well on your way to building a successful and sustainable career as a user-generated content creator.

Focus on quality:

Quality content is essential for building a loyal and engaged audience, so make sure to focus on creating high-quality content that resonates with your audience. This includes using high-quality production values, delivering valuable and informative content, and consistently meeting the needs of your audience.

Diversify your income streams:

Don't rely on a single source of income as a user-generated content creator. Instead, diversify your income streams by exploring a variety of monetization options and seeking out new opportunities as they arise. This can help ensure that you have a stable and sustainable income over the long term.

Build a strong online presence:

Having a strong online presence is essential for building a successful career as a user-generated content creator. This includes building a strong social media following, maintaining a professional website or blog, and leveraging online tools and resources to promote your content.

Network and collaborate:

Building relationships with other creators, influencers, and industry professionals can be a great way to learn from others, share ideas and resources, and grow your audience. Seek out opportunities to network and collaborate with others in your field, and consider joining professional organizations or online communities.

Invest in your education and professional development:

Staying up to date with the latest trends and best practices in the industry is essential for success as a user-generated content creator. Consider investing in your education and professional development by taking courses, attending conferences and events, or working with a mentor or coach.

Remember to stay true to your values and passions, and don't be afraid to take risks and try new things as you grow and evolve in your career.

CONCLUSION

In conclusion, user-generated content is an increasingly important aspect of the online landscape, and there is a growing demand for creators who can produce engaging and authentic content that resonates with their audience. If you have a passion for user-generated content creation and are looking to turn it into a successful career, there are a number of steps you can take to achieve your goals.

First, it's important to understand the basics of user-generated content and its role in the modern digital world. This includes understanding the various platforms and tools available for creating and sharing content, as well as the importance of building and engaging with a community of followers.

Next, you'll want to identify your niche and define your target audience, as this will help you create content that is relevant and resonates with your desired audience. Building your online presence is also key, and this includes leveraging social media platforms to connect with your audience and promote your content. In addition to creating engaging and authentic content, you'll also want to consider the various ways you can monetize your user-generated content, such as through sponsorships and partnerships with brands and companies. Collaborating with others can also be a great way to grow your audience and reach a wider audience.

Stay up to date with the latest trends and best practices in the industry. This can help you stay ahead of the curve and ensure that your content is relevant and engaging. Experiment with different types of content and formats to see what works best for your audience. This could include video, audio, written articles, or other formats. Engage with your audience and encourage them to share their own content and ideas. This can help you build a strong and loyal community of followers. Don't be afraid to try new things and take risks. This is an ever-evolving industry, and being open to new opportunitics and ideas can help you stand out and find success. Network and collaborate with other creators in your niche. This can help you learn from others, share ideas and resources, and potentially reach new audiences.

Seek out opportunities for professional development and education. This could include attending industry conferences and events, taking online courses or workshops, or working with a mentor or coach. Be authentic and genuine in your content. Your audience will appreciate your honesty and authenticity, and it can help you build trust and credibility. Don't be afraid to ask for help or support when you need it. Whether it's seeking advice from colleagues or seeking out resources such as blogs or forums, there are many resources available to help you succeed as a user-generated content creator.

Finally, it's important to stay focused and motivated, as building a successful career as a user-generated content creator takes time and effort. By following these tips and strategies, you'll be well on your way to turning your passion for user-generated content into a successful and fulfilling career. I hope this information has been helpful, and I wish you the best of luck as you embark on your journey as a user-generated content creator. Remember to have fun and enjoy the process, as this is an exciting and rewarding field that offers endless opportunities for creativity and growth. Stay true to yourself and your passions, and you'll be well on your way to building a successful and fulfilling career.

Printed in Poland
by Amazon Fulfillment
Poland Sp. z o.o., Wrocław

30695562R00040